Heroes In History
Inspirational Poems:
15 Black Pioneers For Change

Written by Miriam Moore, Ed.S.
Portraits by Jillian Williams

All rights reserved. Printed in the United States

No part of this book may be reproduced in any form or by any electronic or mechanical means, including information storage and retrieval systems, without the permission in writing from the author. However, reviewers may quote brief passages in a review.

Copyright © 2020 Miriam Moore, Ed.S.

ISBN 978-1-7343610-2-5

Portraits by Jillian Williams
Cover Design by Jo'V
Layout by Remi Bryant

DEDICATION

This book was inspired by my daughter, Serenity, who became interested in these fifteen black heroes at two years old. I dedicate this book to her, my son Brendon, and all young scholars that yearn to learn. These fifteen heroes have done extraordinary things in the world and you can too. Keep dreaming and always remember… You're brave. You're intelligent. You're amazing and you're loved just the way you are.

BARACK OBAMA

His slogan was: YES WE CAN!
In 2008, America voted for this intelligent black man.

With 2 daughters, Malia and Sasha, and Michelle his beautiful spouse,
This senator from Illinois became the first black president elected to the White House.

He wanted affordable health insurance for Americans everywhere,
So he signed a law in 2010 commonly known as "Obamacare."

He won many awards and recognitions, including the Nobel Peace Prize.
Throughout his two terms, many people loved his powerful speeches, and could see passion in his eyes.

That's right, becoming the first black president is quite a change and a victory!
President Obama, #44, is quite a hero in history!

DR. MARTIN LUTHER KING JR.

The man with a dream who said, "Let freedom ring,"
Is none other than the Atlanta-born scholar Dr. ML King.

He believed in equality, and nonviolence too.
He wanted everyone to stick with love, because hate is something we shouldn't do.

Achieving equality and justice is how he dedicated his life.
Through it all, he was supported and encouraged by Coretta, his beautiful wife.

He earned the Nobel Peace Prize, led marches, and gave powerful speeches.
A voice for all Americans... Oh the generations his legacy reaches.

A family man, a mentor, and an awesome preacher, you see...
This dynamic Civil Rights leader is quite a hero in history!

NELSON MANDELA

This Nobel Peace Prize recipient walked amongst us not too long ago.
He led the South African Movement to freedom and loved his people so.

He was an activist that dreamed of a free Africa for many years.
He worked to end unjust laws and believed we could all be liberated from our own fears.

He later became the first black President of South Africa and fought for racial equality.
His intrinsic love for his country and people helped say goodbye to the apartheid policy.

He became an icon of love and peace and taught others how to forgive.
He left a mark on this world in many ways therefore his legacy will always live.

Nelson Mandela's strength, perseverance, and leadership inspired so many.
Affectionately known as "Mandiba," he is quite a hero in history!

ROSA PARKS

A seamstress and an activist who wanted equality for every one of us.
She caught the nation's attention when she refused to give up her seat on a segregated bus.

Go, Rosa! You can't sit here in the front, you must sit in the back!
But Rosa said, "No." She was tired... tired of being mistreated because she was black.

The Montgomery Bus Boycott was sparked because of her brave actions that day.
"We will walk with you," are the words that many people did say.

The bus struggled and the laws were changed because they were simply unfair.
Blacks and whites should have the right to sit, and do it anywhere.

Today we can choose our seats on any bus or public facility, Thanks to the Mother of the Civil Rights Movement who is quite a hero in history!

HARRIET TUBMAN

Originally named Araminta Ross and born as a slave,
She is most remembered for being Harriet Tubman and truly brave.

Young "Minty" was a strong woman that didn't take any mess.
She wanted to escape from the south to freedom, and wouldn't accept anything less.

She was the Underground Railroad conductor who helped hundreds of slaves to flee.
Nicknamed "Moses" because like in the Bible she led her people down the path to be free.

Harriet Tubman not only freed her family, but she also freed hundreds of others.
She risked her life so many times to free many black sisters and brothers.

As an activist, she believed that equal rights for blacks and women was key.
Harriet Tubman, a devoted abolitionist, is quite a hero in history!

SOJOURNER TRUTH

She escaped slavery, and despite being unable to read or write,
She wanted fair treatment for women and African Americans and rose to be a leader in the fight.

Known as a freedom fighter and a traveling Methodist preacher,
She championed the rights of former slaves. Oh Yes she was a people-reacher.

Known as Sojourner Truth, even though her birth name was Isabella Baumfree,
She made her mark all over the U.S. preaching and teaching about the abolition of slavery.

She spent her life spreading her powerful truth no matter what would occur.
She persisted even when many open doors were closed to her.

Known for her perseverance, power, and profound speeches during the nineteenth century,
Sojourner Truth, the feminist and abolitionist, is quite a hero in history!

JACKIE ROBINSON

From a young boy, Jackie dreamed of one day getting in the game.
But baseball in America was not always the same.

His dreams didn't stop just because he was black.
He later stepped on Ebbets Field as a Brooklyn Dodger and never looked back.

He heard the crowd shouting mean things to insult his race.
But with his head held high, he kept running from base to base.

Jackie stood for equality and paved the way for other black players too.
He fought back by playing his best, even when he could hear the crowd's loud boo.

The first African American to play in Major League Baseball helped his team win the World Series...
Persevering and never giving in, is why Jackie Robinson is quite a hero in history!

ELLA FITZGERALD

Ella dreamed of singing and being an entertainer one day,
But since she was black, many clubs would often turn her away.

Persevering and making her dreams come true was her choice.
She kept on singing, and soon enough the country loved her tuneful voice.

"A-Tisket, A-Tasket" was a famous song that she wrote.
Her horn-like voice hit high and very low notes.

She would bebop and scat with so much pizazz.
She became known as the First Lady of Song and the Queen of Jazz.

Ella used her voice to break racial barriers you see.
She won 14 Grammys and is quite a hero in history!

SHIRLEY CHISHOLM

Known for being fearless and outspoken too,
Educator, author, politician...there was so much she could do.

An outspoken political leader in the 60s and 70s,
The first black woman to run for the U.S. Presidency.

As the first black congresswoman, she wasn't always treated nicely.
Racism didn't stop her. She kept fighting for equal rights precisely.

Shirley Chisholm was the first, but she knew she would not be the last.
She sent the message worldwide that times were changing very fast.

Although she didn't win the nomination for the U.S. Presidency,
Her quest for change set dreamers free, making her quite a hero in history!

THURGOOD MARSHALL

As a kid, Thurgood and his dad would sit around and chat.
They would laugh about this and debate about that.

They enjoyed discussing the law, and sometimes their opinions collided.
"When I grow up, I'll be a lawyer." is what Thurgood decided.

He studied and learned the importance of the rule of law,
But while growing up, African Americans being mistreated is something he saw.

He later became a great lawyer with many civil rights cases.
His famous one, Brown vs. Board of Education, put an end to schools being separated by races.

He became the first black Supreme Court Justice in the highest court in the land, "Yippee!"
Uniting people by taking a stand, is why Thurgood Marshall is quite a hero in history!

MARIAN ANDERSON

As a child, young Marian had a voice that could one day wow the nation,
But her family could not afford to get her a formal music education.

Money was later raised for this young dreamer who feared rejection.
She wanted equality for all and dreamed about this correction.

Often turned away for being black, but it didn't stop her singing career.
She knew she was a symbol for her people, and her voice is what the world should hear.

She sang for presidents, thousands at the Lincoln Memorial, and so many more...
The first black to perform with the New York Metropolitan Opera...her voice they all adored.

She broke down racial barriers and was an admired singer of the 20th century.
Marian Anderson, the voice that challenged the nation, is quite a hero in history!

DANIEL HALE WILLIAMS

He was an African American doctor and surgical pioneer.
Despite discrimination, Williams still pursued a medical career.

While in medical school, he opened Provident Hospital, the first to have blacks on staff.
During this time, blacks were refused staff positions, so he made a way on their behalf.

A man with a chest wound was brought in one day seeking medical care.
Williams did surgery on his heart and chest, and successfully repaired the tear.

This successful surgery story only defines Daniel Hale Williams at a glance.
He founded organizations, helped hospitals, and gave many black medical professionals a chance.

Dr. Daniel H. Williams performed the world's first open-heart surgery successfully.
This chief surgeon who paved the way is quite a hero in history!

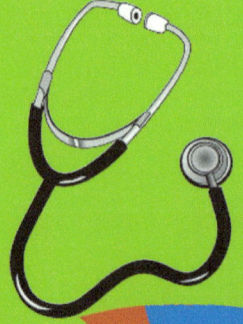

MAE JEMISON

As a child, Mae dreamed about going into space one day.
And she didn't let anyone or anything stand in her way.

She would often gaze at the night sky, because she loved the stars and the moon.
This child with big dreams could see herself becoming a scientist soon.

Not many women or African Americans were scientists when she was a kid.
So working hard and studying science daily is exactly what she did.

Traveling and exploring space is what she would always yearn.
She read a lot, became a doctor, joined NASA and continued to learn.

What being an astronaut in space was really like was no longer a mystery,
Because Mae became the first African-American woman to enter space, so she is quite a hero in history!

BOOKER T. WASHINGTON

Up from slavery and through poverty he came,
Impacting the lives of many who will never forget his name.

Determined to learn and with a goal of education,
He walked miles to achieve his degrees... his legacy impacted the nation.

He was a determined civil rights leader who saw great problems to be solved.
Through his hard work, Tuskegee Institute evolved.

Booker T. Washington became a great speaker and well-known politician,
Improving the lives of African Americans was his sole mission.

The first African American invited to the White House was none other than Mr. Booker T.
This powerful speaker and educator is quite a hero in history!

FREDERICK DOUGLAS

Born into slavery as Frederick Bailey,
He endured many harsh and unbearable treatments daily.

Determined to gain his freedom and take lead,
Douglass learned, and then taught other slaves, how to read.

He disguised as a sailor to escape slavery,
And was one of the courageous few to have such bravery.

Once called the Father of the Civil Rights Movement and a man of great determination,
He believed that America could one day be diverse and free of discrimination.

He spoke about equality and was the first black U.S. Vice President nominee.
Frederick Douglas, the abolitionist, activist, and writer, is quite a hero in history!

COMPREHENSION QUESTIONS

1. Who was the first black president of the United States?

2. Where was Martin Luther King Jr. born?

3. What country did Nelson Mandela become the first black president of?

4. What did Rosa Parks do when asked to change seats?

5. What was Harriet Tubman's role in the Underground Railroad?

6. What was Sojourner Truth's birth name?

7. What is Jackie Robinson most famous for?

8. What famous song did Ella Fitzgerald write?

9. Who was the first black woman to run for US Presidency?

10. What was Thurgood Marshall the first to become?

11. Where was Marian Anderson the first African American to perform?

12. Who performed the first successful open-heart surgery?

13. What did Mae Jemison become the first African American woman to do?

14. What civil rights leader and educator was the first African American invited to the White House?

15. Who was once called the Father of the Civil Rights Movement?

CAN YOU IDENTIFY THE 15 HEROES IN HISTORY

Draw a line matching their picture to their name.

 Martin Luther King Jr.  Harriet Tubman

 Rosa Parks  Jackie Robinson

 Barack Obama  Mae Jemison

 Sojourner Truth  Nelson Mandela

 Booker T. Washington  Ella Fitzgerald

 Marian Anderson  Frederick Douglas

 Thurgood Marshall  Shirley Chisholm

 Daniel Hale Williams

Illustrations © 2020 Miriam Moore

IS THERE ANOTHER HERO IN HISTORY THAT INSPIRES YOU?

Draw a picture and write about him/her.

Share your work with the author using the hashtags
#LearningWithReny
#ReadingWithReny

Illustrations © 2020 Miriam Moore

INSPIRED BY SERENITY MOORE

Serenity Moore is currently a full-time Pre-K student. At the age of two, she became interested in learning about fifteen black leaders after seeing their pictures beautifully displayed on her preschool bulletin board. Her mother, Miriam, took a picture of the bulletin board and began to teach her about these influential black leaders at home. At two years old, Serenity went viral on social media for memorizing and proudly reciting the names of these historic heroes. At three years old, Serenity took her black history lessons with her mom a step further by learning about seven of the fifteen leaders, the impactful African American women. She could even quote each one of them.

Reny, as she's affectionately known, is now four years old and still yearns to learn more about these pioneers for change. Her mom decided to write a short poem about each influential leader to help her and other young children learn about these heroes in history. These fifteen pioneers are among a list of many others, past and present, that made major contributions to the world we live in. Their stories continue to inspire many adults and even children just like young Serenity. Serenity is a precocious child that loves to read, sing, dance, play, and have fun learning. She lives with her father, mother, and big brother, Brendon, in Atlanta, Ga.

@PrincessSerenitySays

ABOUT THE AUTHOR

Miriam Moore is an elementary school teacher and reading specialist. She has an intrinsic love for early literacy and enjoys making learning a fun and engaging experience for all students. She is the founder of Reading Empowers Neighborhood Youth (R.E.N.Y.), a company that spreads the joy of reading through bookish apparel, donates books, and supports a variety of literacy initiatives in low income communities around the world. She enjoys spending quality time with her family and teaching children how to be lifelong learners. She is happily married to her college sweetheart, Rev. Brandon M. Moore. Together they have two beautiful children, Brendon and Serenity.

@MMOORE1908

ABOUT THE ARTIST

"Representation matters" and that is what Jillian Williams wants her art to portray. Jillian aspires to create art that her childhood self could view and not only feel inspired by, but could see herself in. As a visual artist based in Atlanta, Georgia, Jillian creates vibrant portraits primarily with acrylic paints on canvas. She describes herself as a small town girl with big dreams and hopes to inspire the child in us all.

@BECOMING_JILLIE

REFERENCES

Anderson, Marian. Facts for Kids. Kiddle Encyclopedia. https://kids.kiddle.com/Marian_Anderson

Biography.com Editors. A&E Television Networks . (2019). Daniel Hale Williams Biography. https://www.biography.com/scientist/daniel-hale-williams

Brinkley, Douglas. (2000). Rosa Parks: A Life. New York: Viking Penguin.

Brown, Lauren, & Lenny, Hort. (2006). Nelson Mandela: A Photographic Story of a Life. New York: DK Publishing.

Dougherty, Steve. (2009). Hopes and Dreams: The Story of Barack Obama. New York: Black Dog & Leventhal.

Douglas, Frederick. (2004). Narrative of the Life of Frederick Douglass. Cheswold, DE: Prestwick House.

Nelson, Ken. (Accessed 6 January 2020). "Biography: Harriet Tubman for Kids." Ducksters, Technological Solutions, Inc. (TSI), www.ducksters.com/biography/women_leaders/harriet_tubman.php.

Nelson, Ken. (Accessed 6 January 2020). "Biography: Jackie Robinson." Ducksters, Technological Solutions, Inc. (TSI), www.ducksters.com/sports/jackie_robinson.php.

Nelson, Ken. (Accessed 6 January 2020). "Biography: Booker T. Washington for Kids." Ducksters, Technological Solutions, Inc. (TSI), www.ducksters.com/biography/booker_t_washington.php.

Roop, Peter, & Connie Roop. (2002). Sojourner Truth. New York: Scholastic.

Schwartz, Alison Mundy. (1999). A century of great African Americans / Alison Mundy Schwartz. - New York : Gramercy Books.

Shepherd, Jodie. (2015). Mae Jemison (Rookie Biographies). Children's Press

www.ingramcontent.com/pod-product-compliance
Lightning Source LLC
Chambersburg PA
CBHW042248100526
44587CB00002B/71